ART AND
IN D

T0246366

Marc Camille Chaimowicz
Sketch of the Armadillo House

**MARC CAMILLE CHAIMOWICZ
ROGER DIENER**

Marc Camille Chaimowicz
Sketches faxed to Diener & Diener

Diener & Diener
Digital studies of Chaimowicz's patterns (enlarged)

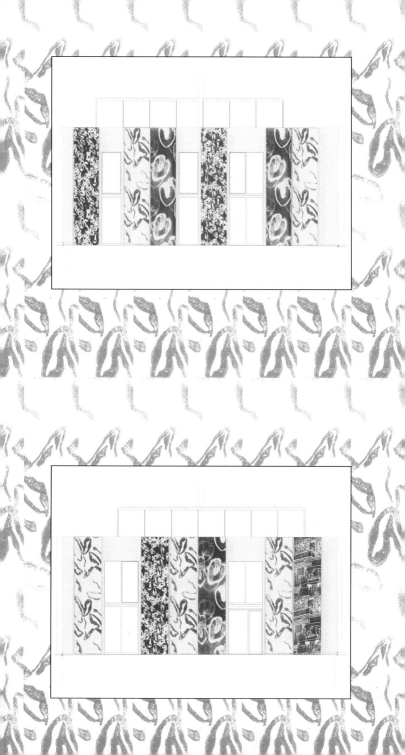

Manufacturing process, pp. 6, 8, 9, 10, 14, 30, 43

The volume in your hands is a fresh start for the book series "Art and Architecture in Discussion", which fosters discussion among disciplines – art and architecture in particular, but also design, fashion and film. I launched the series 23 years ago with a dialogue between Frank O. Gehry and Kurt W. Forster with the wonderful support of the then director of the Kunsthaus Bregenz, Edelbert Köb. At that time I did not anticipate the large response the book series would enjoy. Fourteen volumes have since been published, all with renowned artists, architects and designers. The series went into hibernation for some years, but the enthusiasm of Fredi Fischli and Niels Olsen inspired me to relaunch it. We are extremely pleased to have Franz König on board as our new publisher.

It is a pleasure and honour to continue the series in conversation with the London-based artist Marc Camille Chaimowicz, the Swiss architect Roger Diener and the author Maryam Diener. The discussion focuses in particular on the fascinating and unique Armadillo House, truly a Gesamtkunstwerk.

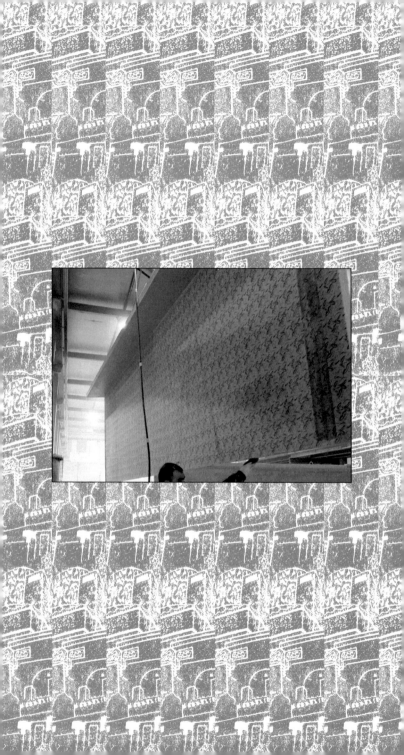

We have long followed the work of Diener & Diener and it came as a surprise to learn that Maryam and Roger Diener planned to build their own home in collaboration with the artist Marc Camille Chaimowicz. Rather than striving to build a "Meisterhaus" – an idealised representation of Diener & Diener's architectural programme – they joined forces with someone who seems at first sight to be a most unlikely contributor to their project. The collaboration between artist and architect has led to a result that goes far beyond conventional parameters. One might compare it to the surrealist game of the exquisite corpse, in which autonomous parts come together and form a single whole, though without striving to merge the separate voices. Unlike the surrealist game, however, fostering the autonomy of the other, in this case Kunst am Bau (art for architecture), requires precise planning. Paradoxically, freedom thrives within a strict set of rules.

Chaimowicz claims the interior as a pictorial space while also referencing the history of architecture, art and design. His agenda has been described as the celebration of domestic detritus and his spatial installations appear as painterly tableaus. From the 1970s onwards he advanced a critique of rigid, austere minimalism, as in *Enough Tiranny*. For Diener, on the other hand, pictorial space is not a factor. Instead, he puts forward a modernist notion of non-expression, with architecture functioning as its raw material. In his architecture, it is not the insertion of culturally codified images but rather spatial configurations that shape the movement and circulation of inhabitants.

Another source of tension can be observed between the two protagonists. Diener & Diener's work expresses longevity; large-scale intervention in cities built of stone are the core of their work. Architecture is a slow practice and urban planning, a long-term process that is shaped by the constraints of politics and finance. By contrast, Chaimowicz's art is mostly embedded in the short-term context of the exhibition; it is temporary, ephemeral, performative and – most importantly –

Marc Camille Chaimowicz
Enough Tiranny
Serpentine Gallery, London, 1972

fanciful, which could, under certain circumstances, be the architect's ultimate enemy.

Ordinarily, Diener & Diener do not build private homes and, even when working on a single building, they tend to map out an urbanist strategy. So we were particularly interested in finding out what motivated the architects to work with an artist so consistently focused on the intimacy of interiors. A look at earlier collaborations is revealing, such as Helmut Federle's contributions to the Swiss embassy in Berlin and the building for Novartis in Basel or, more recently, the work of several artists for the Swiss Re Next building in Zürich. Federle clad the entire Novartis building with layered sheets of coloured glass, demonstrating how eminently suited Diener & Diener's understated architecture is as a vehicle for artists.

It was with such juxtapositions in mind and a deep appreciation of both architect and artist that we undertook to visit Armadillo House. As we walked up the hill overlooking Basel, we saw the recently completed home come into view. It stood out like an industrial building in the middle of a residential area. The house stands close to the street instead of being nestled in an impressive front yard. The initial impression from afar is that of an automobile repair shop in a Milanese suburb. As you come closer, vertical, concrete slabs subvert this impression, their appearance communicating a certain elegance and even an ambiguous classicism. The light colouring of the extremely subtle ornamentation becomes visible between trees planted so close to the building that they almost seem to attack the façade.

Marc Camille Chaimowicz has masked the concrete slabs with a pattern that looks like wallpaper, giving each slab its own colour and motif. It is as if the house had been turned inside out, its domesticity conveyed by ornaments that seem to "unhouse" this home. This large-scale intervention is not visible from afar. Since it is only perceived from nearby, Chaimowicz's cladding reinforces the sense of exposed intimacy and makes manifest the subtle interaction of art and architecture.

This inversion lends the building a subversive tension, where the basically unbroken façade becomes a subtle travesty of domesticity. No windows have been cut into the patterned wall, which would have provided a framed gaze from the street into the interior. Instead, the artist signifies the interior by employing the traditional decorative technique of painting walls with a stencilled linoleum roller – a method used by the Wiener Werkstätte to imitate wallpaper by applying real paint. The soft coat of paint on the harsh concrete foundation is almost like a garment, dressing the raw, shed-like architecture in a translucent light.

In our conversations with Chaimowicz, he explained that he was curious about the relationship between Roger and Maryam because he understands his practice as a form of portraiture – expanded portraiture, as it were, in which displacement is immanent and the subject therefore need not make a literal appearance. As he puts it, "Jean Cocteau doesn't appear in the work of Jean Cocteau." It is thus only logical that, instead of preserving a phantom mapped out with historical accuracy, Chaimowicz stages Cocteau's bedroom as a museum installation, a room within a room. In this sense, Armadillo House is a portrait of Maryam and Roger.

The intimacy of the artist's approach is also reflected in the way he works. Chaimowicz does not have a big studio and he shies away from the tendency of many artists to produce huge amounts of work with the help of numerous assistants. He works slowly, on his own, responding to specific situations and not recycling what has gone before. He invests a great deal in his exhibitions, essentially creating a Gesamtkunstwerk destined to vanish again within just a few weeks or months. He has thus turned his attention increasingly to commissioned works and projects that have a degree of permanence.

Marc Camille Chaimowicz's work on Armadillo House went well beyond the façade. Collaborating with Diener & Diener meant benefitting from their experience with a wide range of materials, including wood, fabric, tiles, metal, glass and many more. In addition, thanks to the studio's professional database book Chaimowicz had the opportunity to call on first-rate craftsmen. Working closely with Maryam Diener, he designed such items for the interior as floor tiles, the kitchen, lamps and a sculptural railing, creating a counterpoint to the clear structure of the architecture. Having no individual rooms, the open floor plan of the house shows a simplicity that welcomes Chaimowicz's multifaceted interior design. In the kitchen, wall-mounted plates found at the flea market stand in contrast to painted cupboards with crystalline glass door knobs and custom-made floor tiles. The second floor is conceived as a gallery with an ornamental railing. It extends across the whole house so that Chaimowicz's lamps hang suspended through the entire height of the building. Armadillo House is thus animated by the fruitful push and pull between artistic and architectural practices, creating an atmosphere of enigmatic tension for its inhabitants.

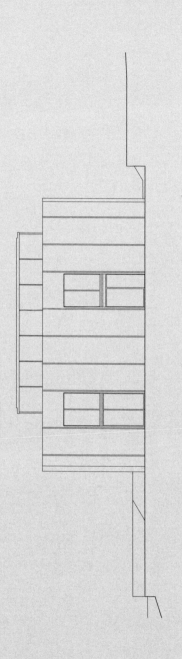

WEST

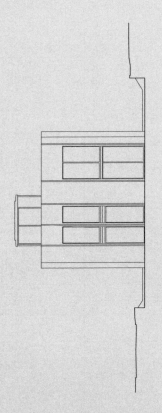

SOUTH

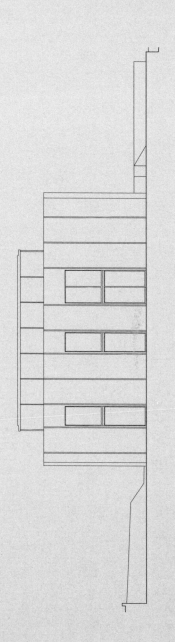

EAST

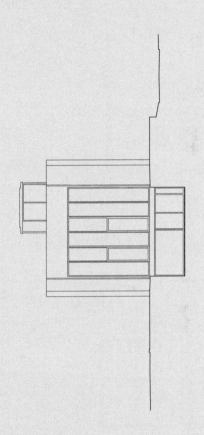

NORTH

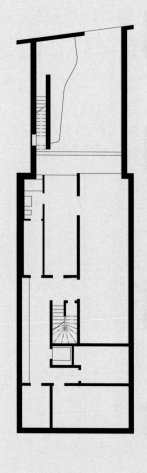

BASEMENT

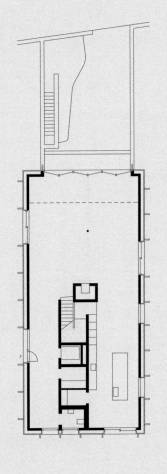

GROUND FLOOR

1 FLOOR

2 FLOOR

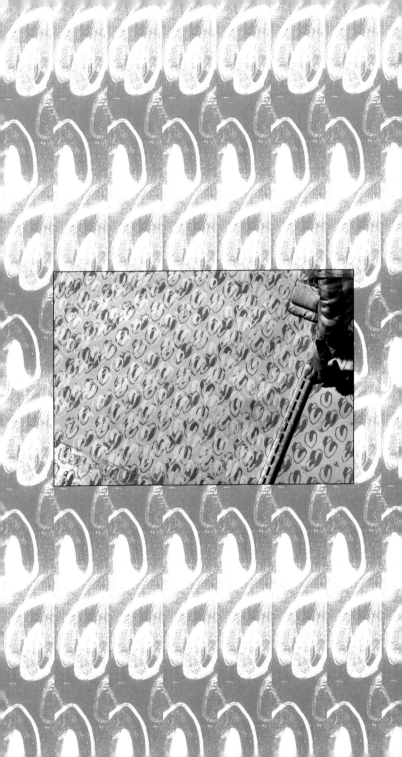

MARC CAMILLE CHAIMOWICZ (MCC)
AND ROGER DIENER (RD)

A CONVERSATION WITH

CRISTINA BECHTLER (CB)
FREDI FISCHLI (FF)
NIELS OLSEN (NO)

FF We want to begin with the question: what attracted you to each other's work? What you each do seems very different at first glance, not just your discipline, but the aesthetic as well. Roger, I see your approach to architecture as essentialist or non-expressive, while you, Marc Camille, deal with the notion of ornament, décor and a certain opulence. We are therefore curious to hear how your – in our opinion surprising – collaboration for the Armadillo House in Basel came about.

MCC Well, we first crossed paths at an event about the new headquarters for Swiss Re, where Roger gave a presentation. I was singularly impressed, not just by how ambitious the project was, but also by the ideology behind the building. For instance, Roger had commissioned a detailed sociological study of the staff at Swiss Re, acquiring insights that informed his design and allowed him to take a very perceptive approach to the building and accommodate its actual day-to-day functions. So, I was intrigued. But it never occurred to me that we might work together. Then I heard that Roger was giving a talk at the Barbican in London. I got there a bit early and was sitting in the lobby when someone called me by my first name. It was Roger, and he was delighted to see me. He asked me to join them for dinner afterwards. When I learned that they were in London almost every other weekend, I invited them to my new apartment in Vauxhall and there he informally mentioned the project for a new house in Basel. I had become more dissatisfied with the pressure of having an international profile and had decided to take a year off, so the timing was perfect. Obviously, I was interested; this was a once in a lifetime opportunity. How could one pass it up?

Diener & Diener
Swiss Re Next
Zürich, 2008–2017

NO Just shortly before you had realised a commission in Vauxhall – an intervention in the design of the new building housing the Cabinet Gallery.

Trevor Horne Architects
Cabinet Gallery
London, 2016

Vauxhall was quite different. I should first point out that **MC** Cabinet designed it themselves. Martin McGeown and Andrew Wheatley basically designed the whole building in consultation with Charles Asprey, who provided the financial backing, and of course Trevor Horne and his team. So, many people were involved in the building's design with the greatest input coming from Cabinet. I sat in on a few meetings, but I wasn't that directly involved. They wanted three artists to contribute to the design of the building. I was one of them. The others were Lucy McKenzie who did the decorative panel work on the balconies, and John Knight who did this one window on the ground floor – a very subtle, but important intervention that acknowledges the function of the building and enables an architectural feature leading directly into the gallery, like a Barnett Newman "zip". I was invited to design the window frames.

NO Yes, they have an irregular, angular wooden structure, making each individual window painterly, recalling a modernist tableau.

Marc Camille Chaimowicz
Model for a Window
2015

Designing the windows was one reason I got involved. The other **MC** was personal. I was looking to move for various reasons, not **C** least health-related, because I knew that at some point I would no longer be able to live where I had lived for more than 30 years – on the top floor of a 1900 building without a lift. This seemed to be a great opportunity to downsize. So I approached the gallery, who were actually interested in having one of their artists live above the gallery. I was fortunate enough to have an architect friend Stephen Beasley help me design the interior space since I was acquiring only the shell of a flat. That was really exciting. I got closely involved in the floor plan, the finishing and the redrawing of the apartment even though I have very little architectural experience.

NO Was this your first permanent architectural intervention?

It certainly was. It was unique in that sense and also because the **MC C**
collaboration was so intense, the fact that we were almost co-au-
thoring a project. I had not been involved to such a degree before.

FF It would be interesting to hear from you Roger. How would you
characterise the Vauxhall building when you first visited?

When Maryam and I first approached the building in Vauxhall, **RD**
it was very clear to us that it was both an interesting and com-
plex collaboration. On the one hand, it was completely different
from traditional housing, yet on the other hand, not as spectac-
ular as one might expect from its description. I did not realise,
for example, how special the windows are until coming back
from the pub one day and seeing the building from another
angle. It's a great neighbourhood. There is a little city farm
across the street. You feel the neighbourhood spirit; there's an
energy and an incredible sense of community. In a way, the
building, in all its complexity, is an unexpected but elegant response to all of the informally organised structures nearby.

MC C It is most interesting to walk around the building with Roger
because he has a particular eye for public housing which, as we
know, requires great commitment and experience. For instance,
in the bedroom of my apartment there is a really wonderful
view which is layered almost like a theatre set; in the foreground
there is a great Victorian school building. Farther back there is
social housing from the 50s to the 70s and then, in the distant
background, there is the 21st century – the city of London with
the Richard Rogers buildings, etc. So you have three centuries
in one view, a wonderful context.

How interesting, when you talk about the building now, you **NO**
really address it from an urban perspective, how it is situated
in the cityscape, but your work is all about the interior, domesticity and the history of design. Roger, it is obvious from your
oeuvre that you have always resisted working in domestic pri-

vate spaces. I was wondering, what made you decide to focus more on public projects rather than private villas?

Diener & Diener
Apartment Buildings Hammerstrasse
Basel, 1978–1981

RD An architect's oeuvre has a lot to do with the opportunities that present themselves. As a young architect, you can't be choosy. We were privileged to be commissioned for the subsidised housing project Hammerstrasse in Basel already in the second half of the 70s and this project defined our practice for the first 15 years. An invitation to an international competition for housing in Salzburg followed and added to our early reputation as architects engaged in housing. At that time Salzburg was a hotspot within the debate on contemporary architecture and all of a sudden, we found ourselves among the likes of such important architects as Luigi Snozzi and Alvaro Siza. Following Salzburg, we were invited to international housing competitions in Amsterdam and elsewhere, mainly based on the transformation of former industrial sites such as factories or breweries. Only later did we become involved in public projects like the extension of the Swiss embassy in Berlin, but I was always hesitant about the programme of private villas. Either you design a house as a strong answer to the programme, a signature statement the client might be fond of, or you try to give shape to the specific visions clients have for their house. I was not attracted by either concept. There are still other productive options but they have to be based on mutual curiosity and trust.

Diener & Diener
Warteckhof
Basel, 1992–1996

In 1995 you and Martin Steinmann published a book titled *Das* **NO**
Haus und die Stadt.

RD Yes, it actually became a reference book because it was an at-
tempt to discuss urban planning concepts in terms of the poten-
tial of urban and architectural design, and included documen-
tation of case studies as well as built projects. This message was
proposed at a crucial moment in the debate and therefore the
response was quite strong. Such projects imply a certain scale,
like university buildings, office buildings or housing. At that
time villas seemed far removed from our practice.

Diener & Diener
University Building
Malmö, 2003–2005

So what gave you the courage to build your first private home **CB**
in Basel?

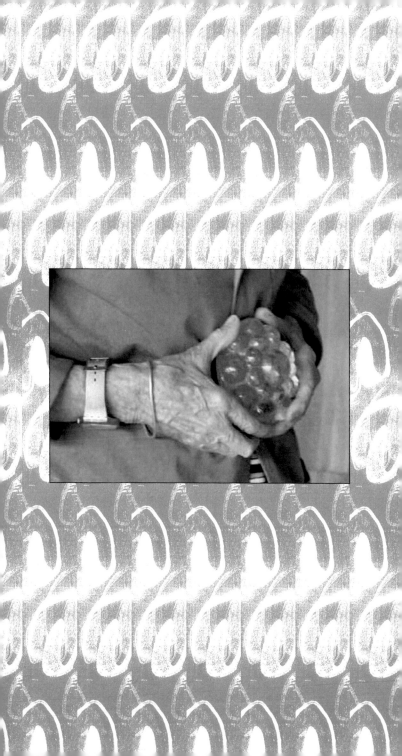

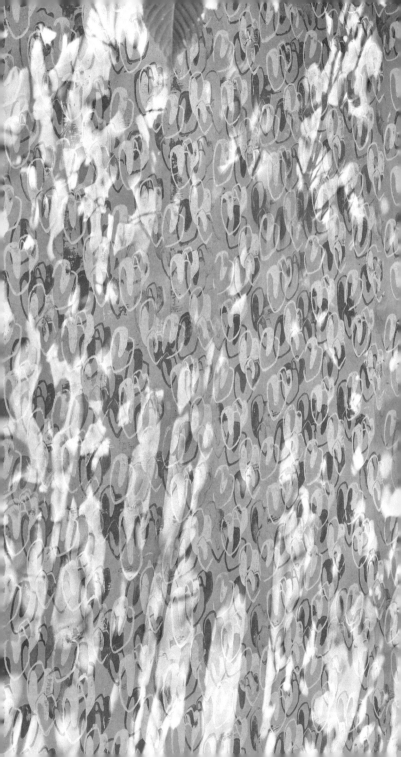

RD It was more out of weakness than courage. {Laughter} It was Maryam's influence. She wanted me to do it; I was really not prepared.

The way you dealt with this problem is impressive because the **NO** area where your house is located is full of relatively conventional villas with gardens in front. Your project has an industrial feel to it. No garden in front, but instead a garage.

FF You said that you were always more interested in houses that have to do with work. That's clearly reflected in the looks of this home, which is presumably both for living and working.

Yes, home plus studio appeals to me much more than a mono- **RD** functional residential villa. In a way, it's a cross between an elegant Italian villa and a rundown industrial structure. And of course, architecture always has references, an architectural past. It's a question of composition and has nothing to do with being postmodern or not. In St. Alban-Tal, for instance, we introduced studios on the ground floor even though the competition did not call for them. That was really early in 1983/84. We analysed the area with its late medieval buildings and early industrial paper mills. Our competition included aspects of industrial design combined with the vocabulary of Gothic architecture, but it was less about collage, as Martin Steinmann suggests, but rather about the complexity of composition. It is not just a matter of combining visual experiences but creating a compelling and inseparable whole.

Diener & Diener
Apartment Buildings St. Alban-Tal
Basel, 1981–1986

CB How did you have the courage to hand over important aesthetic decisions to Marc Camille? Did you take decisions together for the design of the Armadillo House?

An artist's work should have a crucial influence on the gestalt **RD** of a building. In my experience, those projects in which the artistic work has become prominent have proved to be particularly interesting.

So, yes, we took the decisions together as far as the scope and mapping of the artwork for the house is concerned. However, this did not concern the artwork itself. It was, of course, solely up to Marc Camille, and all parts were realised exactly as he developed and presented them.

Marc Camille Chaimowicz
Your Place or Mine …
Jewish Museum, New York, 2018

It starts with the architectural design, with the three-dimensional organisation of a programme in space. Design is the foundation of dialogue between artist and architect.

The architect is, of course, solely responsible for the function, unless the functional design is also included in the dialogue between artist and architect. But that was not the case with the Armadillo House. I suggested Marc Camille work on the parts of the project where our repertoire as architects was exhausted. His approach not only adds expressive surfaces but even shapes the architectural space. The overall (in contrast to the specific) nature of the space, the transparency of the space, an important

quality for me, would not be destroyed or drowned out. On the contrary.

The high walls and floor are transformed into a gentle embrace by the presence of Marc Camille's work, which softens the rawness of their proportions.

This illustrates the special challenge of a collaboration between artist and architect. It can only be fruitful if the work of both merges into a whole and yet both parts are able to retain their autonomous form. Finding these fields is the focus of the dialogue. It involves conceptual questions as well as those of the actual realisation of the artistic work as a constituent of the building.

The involvement of a prominent artistic work that essentially shapes the design of the building and at the same time ensures the autonomy of architecture and art is also the foundation of dialogue in the projects we have realised with Helmut Federle.

Diener Federle Wiederin
Novartis Campus Forum 3
Basel, 2002–2005

FRAME MUSTARD
BASE PUTTY
M PASTEL GREEN
+ BLUSH
R CORAL

FRAME BLUSH
BASE SATIN
M KHAKI
R PUTTY

B1A

B1B

Marc Camille Chaimowicz
Design of tiles for ceramicist

FRAME LAVENDER
BASE PASTEL GREEN
+ BLUSH
M SAFFRON
R KHAKI

FRAME SATIN
BASE CHAMPAGNE
M BLUSH
R WARM GREYS

B1C

B1D

BLUSH

Diener & Diener
Swiss Embassy
West wall by Helmut Federle
Berlin, 1995–2000

NO Marc Camille, I see your ornamental pattern on the façade of the Armadillo House as a reverse side of the interior. The patterns you applied to the raw concrete panels recall tapestries, which are common in old-fashioned interior spaces. Now, it seems as if the volume has been turned inside out and, in an abstract way, the intimate language of the domestic is made public. What made you decide on a patterned façade?

It came out of dialogues with Roger and Maryam. What is ironic about this collaboration is that I was so busy that year – I had three solo shows – that I was forced to change the way I work. The dilemma for me is that when I am invited to do a show, people increasingly presume that I will deliver a newly conceived work. This is partly my own doing because I tend to respond specifically to given spaces, I don't recycle old works per se. Given the way I work, this became untenable. I work alone, I don't have a big studio, and I work slowly; I am the antithesis to that American way of working, those production lines producing lots and lots of works with a massive team and assistants. I always put so much effort into a show, like the one at Indipendenza in Rome, and then after six weeks it's gone. I started to question that dynamic and became increasingly interested in working through commissions or on projects that would have a degree of permanence. So, as mentioned, the timing was perfect for me.

But in terms of the outside, my input was relatively small because we were working with pre-existing design decisions. Once again, the idea for the façade arose from conversations

Marc Camille Chaimowicz
Design of tiles for ceramicist

with Roger and Maryam during their visit to my apartment in Vauxhall. They went into one of the rooms, actually the most private of the apartment, the bedroom, and Roger noticed straight away that I had added a patina to one of the concrete walls. Of course, that must have rung a bell. But the more recent decisions that we took had to do with the intimate space of the interior and its fabric, the floor, the decorations for the kitchen cupboards, and how to finish off the bedroom. Some decisions were taken about the exterior, the metal gates and the glass ornaments above the window frames. I mean, we were working with quite a wide range of materials. The balustrade on the first floor was a remarkable piece of engineering. What I found particularly interesting about this project was that Roger has so many connections. So, I was able to take short cuts and delegate tasks to the very best craftspeople, something which I am not always able to do.

Interior of Marc Camille
Chaimowicz's apartment

FF It would be interesting to learn more about the sources and references that informed your interventions in the Armadillo House. The installations in your exhibitions are often very beautiful, but at the same time, they have an uncanny side to them. Every object is so charged and comes with its distinctive history of which the viewer is unaware.

I am pleased you noticed that! From the start I was very conscious **MC** of the relationship between Roger and Maryam – so the project **C** was a form of portraiture. In several works around portraiture that interest me, the subject is not actually visible. For instance, Jean Cocteau doesn't appear in the work "*Jean Cocteau...*" and *The Casting of the Maids* doesn't feature the work of Jean Genet. Yet with the Armadillo House, I see it as kind of a portrait about two people who will use that space as their personal living space.

Marc Camille Chaimowicz
The Casting of the Maids...
Digital video, 2012

CB This is very interesting because you are also known for criticising modernist architecture, for example, as "inhuman". Yet, I would say that Roger falls in the modernist architect tradition.

We spoke openly about these issues, and I share Marc Camille's **RD** critique of contemporary architecture, and also modern architecture, for its male-focused gestures. I think that we addressed this issue in Binningen. When you look at those façade panels now, there is a feminine quality to them. They are fabulously fragile and soft – characteristics you would never expect from slabs of concrete.

FF Marc Camille's subversive intervention triggers thought, raises questions.

I think Roger's subtle reference to the subject of gender is very **MCC** relevant because I have long felt that my decorative commentary feminised the building. Once during a project meeting, I suggested to Roger that he should introduce me as his couturier at the next meeting, since I was, in essence, dressing the building.

RD The panelling with those mere six-centimetre-thick concrete slabs enhances this notion of "dressing". It is apparent that they are

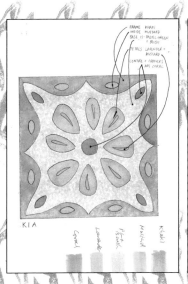

FRAME KHAKI
INSIDE MUSTARD
BASE IS PASTEL GREEN
+ BLUSH
PETALS LAVENDER +
MUSTARD
CENTRE + CORNERS
ARE CORAL

KIA

Coral   Lavender   Pastel Blush   Mustard   Khaki

FRAME CORAL
INSIDE SAFFRON
BASE IS KHAKI +
PETALS BLUSH +
CORAL
CENTRE CORAL
CORNERS MUSTARD

KIB

Marc Camille Chaimowicz
Design of tiles for ceramicist

FRAME LAVENDER
AND PUTTY
BASE KHAKI AND
CORAL
PETALS MUSTARD
AND KHAKI
CENTRE CORAL

KIC

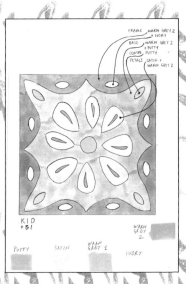

FRAME WARM GREY 2
+ IVORY
BASE WARM GREY 1
+ PUTTY
CENTRE PUTTY
PETALS SATIN +
WARM GREY 2

KID
+ 51

WARM
GREY
2

PUTTY   SATIN   WARM GREY 1   IVORY

organised in such a way that they aren't load bearing. Marc Camille has always shown his pattern-based artworks within interiors. But the second "bell", so to speak, or another moment when the idea for the façade came up, was when I discovered your series of works consisting of panels with different tapestries, propped loosely against the wall. I could easily imagine such works outdoors as well. Quite interesting is that some of your panels have a painted pattern, but others are actually marble plates.

CB I remember your exhibition at the National Gallery in Berlin (2008), where you installed your panels leaning on Mies van der Rohe's precious green marble walls. I read this as a critical gesture.

RD Our intention was to create a façade that almost appears to be a curtain, to have a textile quality to it. This was a perfect fit for Binningen.

CB The two of you hadn't seen the panels in Berlin?

Marc Camille Chaimowicz
For MvdR
5th Berlin Biennial for Contemporary Art,
Neue Nationalgalerie Berlin, 2008

RD No, I wish we had. You know the first thing Marc Camille said was that he would like his patterns to be visible only as you come closer to the house. At first, I thought: Oh, no I don't want

Marc Camille Chaimowicz
Design of kitchen countertop

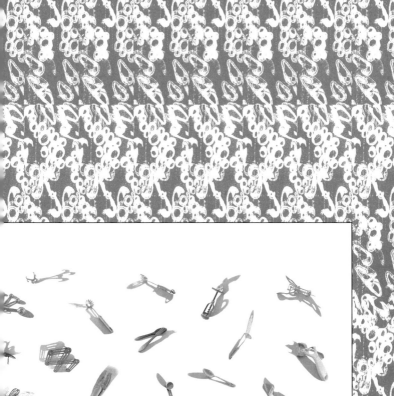

it to be so subtle, but in the end, it turned out exactly like Marc Camille suggested.

I would like to come back to the notion of portraiture you **NO** mentioned before, Marc Camille. Some of your early installations of interior spaces were dedicated to literary protagonists. Did you also work on Maryam and Roger's project in a narrative manner or is there a literary source?

MC Rather than going back to earlier works, let me speak about the
C Armadillo House. The process was as follows: Roger would examine the plans and the various proposed requirements for a period of time, after which I would consider other possibilities and come back to him with some new drawings. Then we would discuss my suggestions, some of which would then be modified in the process. The longer we worked together, the more the process improved. I got to know Roger and Maryam better and better, and my perception of their relationship is reflected in my work. This work is not transferable, it is unique to the two of them. This is what I mean about portraiture being specific.

In this sense, it is a literary portrait. **CB**

MC Yes, in a way. Some specificities, like for example my unrealised
C idea to depict the initials of Maryam and Roger on the façade of the building, actually came from my fabric design of the curtains. Some subtle jokes also appear, like the "Pour Roger" in the textile ornament.

But other people are also involved, not just the two of you. **FF**

RD May I say that your dialogue with Maryam was particularly intense. I was not always part of the dialogue, but the conversations we had with you were very inspiring. They went far beyond choice of fabric or colour. You contributed a lot with your French cultural background and that certainly influenced the dialogue as well. There was much to discuss in the designing of 23 different floor tiles! {Laughter}.

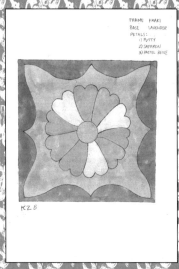

FRAME PASTEL GREEN
+ BLUSH
BASE SATIN
PETALS 1. SAFFRON
2. KHAKI
CORAL X
CENTRE SATIN

KZA
*+B3A

SAFFRON   SATIN

FRAME KHAKI
BASE LAVENDER
PETALS:
1) PUTTY
2) SAFFRON
3) PASTEL BEIGE

KZB

Marc Camille Chaimowicz
Design of tiles for ceramicist, pp. 77, 79.

FRAME SAFFRON
BASE + MUSTARD
CENTRE
PETALS:
1) BLUEBELL +?
2) CORAL
3) KHAKI

KZC

BLUEBELL

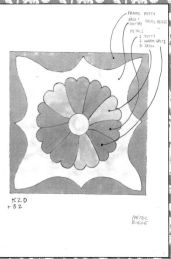

FRAME PUTTY
BASE + PASTEL BEIGE
CENTRE
PETALS
1. PUTTY
2. WARM GREY?
3. SATIN

KZD
+B2

PASTEL
BIEGE

When I was studying in London in the 1960s – first at Ealing, then Camberwell and then the Slade, three very different schools – the dominant role models were principally minor figurative painters from the "London School". Naturally I disagreed with this premise and looked to the Americans for an alternative. I was sceptical of the conventions in British institutions, especially for ideological but also cultural and personal reasons. Partly because I have no English DNA in my family, I was drawn to the European sensibility as a possible third alternative. The European tradition with its surrealists, its symbolists and of course its literature resonated the most for me, and it is in this tradition that I find the majority of my references, especially in terms of literature, film and the visual arts. I also immersed myself in the Viennese sensibility by choosing to live there for a period of time. England didn't feel like home for me, so I was searching for an appropriate spiritual alternative. I obviously have kind of detached and romantic ideas of Europe, evidenced by the Viennese and Parisian references in Binningen. These two cultural histories are the richest for me to draw upon, especially in the decorative arts. England only has Bloomsbury art or William Morris to offer, and I am greatly sceptical of both, William Morris in particular. So, one must look for alternatives. This is why Roger Diener's contributions are so vital.

Marc Camille Chaimowicz
Enough Tiranny
Serpentine Gallery, London, 1972

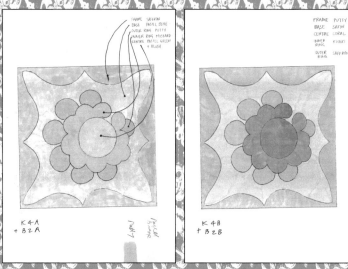

K4A
FRAME SAFFRON
BASE PASTEL BLUE
OUTER RING PUTTY
INNER RING MUSTARD
CENTRE PASTEL GREEN + BLUSH

K4A
+ B2A

K4B
FRAME PUTTY
BASE SATIN
CENTRE CORAL
INNER RING KHAKI
OUTER RING SAFFRON

K4B
+ B2B

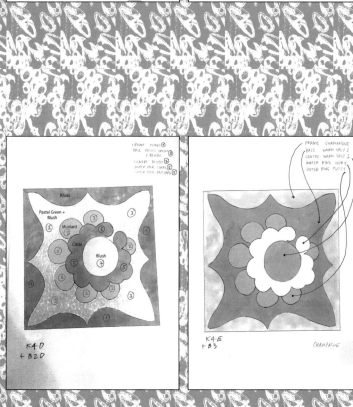

K4D
FRAME KHAKI ④
BASE PASTEL GREEN + BLUSH ③
CENTRE BLUSH ⑤
INNER RING CORAL ⑥
OUTER RING MUSTARD ②

Khaki
Pastel Green + Blush
Mustard
Coral
Blush

K4D
+ B2D

K4E
FRAME CHAMPAGNE
BASE WARM GREY 2
CENTRE WARM GREY 1
INNER RING IVORY
OUTER RING PUTTY

K4E
+ B3

CHAMPAGNE

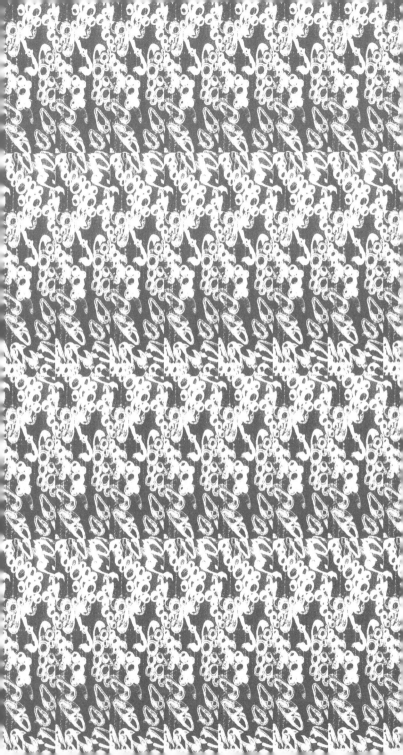

FF What you describe sounds so romantic, yet often in your exhibitions I sense that you are suppressing things. There are so many undercurrents: sexuality, references to literature, the symbolism of the furniture and models. Furthermore, for viewers, interiors that aren't your own can be intimidating. You don't know their history.

I think both Roger and I choose to step back. I always keep my **MC** artwork at a distance. My work is never about self-portraiture; **C** that is clear.

NO I think this distance also characterises the way Roger works with artists. In preparing for this interview we talked about this romantic notion of architects and artists collaborating, but there's so much more to it.

Mutual respect and open dialogue.   **CB**

RD It's more you know, there is indeed a romantic element, you have to love and trust one another. At every step of the way you need to consider whether a decision favours one over the other. This is key, and it makes the process dynamic and peaceful at the same time.

I really had a good feeling when I noticed that Roger wears his **MC** watch on the right wrist just as I do. **C**

Marc Camille Chaimowicz,
Designs for lift, pp. 89, 92–94

Texts
Cristina Bechtler, Marc Camille Chaimowicz, Roger Diener,
Fredi Fischli, Niels Olsen

Edited by
Cristina Bechtler, Fredi Fischli and Niels Olsen

Special thanks to
Maryam Diener
Diener & Diener
Anna Clifford, Studio of Marc Camille Chaimowicz

Editing and copyediting
Catherine Schelbert and Elizabeth MacFadyen

Book Design
Teo Schifferli

Photographs of Diener & Diener buildings
courtesy Diener & Diener; p. 42 photograph top: Bernhard
Strauss; p. 42 photograph bottom: Gerry Johansson;
p. 58 photograph: Christian Richters

Photographs of works by Marc Camille Chaimowicz
courtesy of the artist and Cabinet London; p. 68 photograph:
Jason Larkin

Printed and bound by
DZA Druckerei zu Altenburg

www.buchhandlung-walther-koenig.de
verlag@buchhandlung-walther-koenig.de

Printed in Germany

Bibliographic information published by the Deutsche Nationalbibliothek. The Deutsche Nationalbibliothek lists this publication in the Deutsche Nationalbibliografie; detailed bibliographic data are available in the Internet at http://dnb.d-nb.de.

Distribution

Buchhandlung Walther König Ehrenstrasse 4
D – 50672 Köln
T +49 (0) 221/20 59 6 53
verlag@buchhandlung-walther-koenig.de

ISBN 978-3-7533-0248-5